Are Your Affairs in Order?

A Planning Guide and Resource Book

OLDER ADULT ISSUES SERIES

The Office of Older Adult Ministry of the Presbyterian Church (U.S.A.) and Geneva Press are grateful for the generous gifts of many individuals, congregations, and organizations that helped make possible the publication of this series.

Are Your Affairs in Order?

A Planning Guide and Resource Book

Senior Adult Council
Byrn Mawr Presbyterian Church
Bryn Mawr, Pennsylvania

Published for the Office of Older Adult Ministry,
A Ministry of the General Assembly Council,
Presbyterian Church (U.S.A.)

Geneva Press
Louisville, Kentucky

ISBN 0-664-50085-4

Contents

Introduction

This book was prepared by the Senior Adult Council of the Bryn Mawr Presbyterian Church, Bryn Mawr, Pennsylvania, for use by members of the Presbyterian Church (U.S.A.). Its purpose is to encourage and assist you to plan ahead, thereby minimizing the stress of unexpected events. We hope you will take advantage of the many resources available in the church and the community so that you may maintain a high quality of life as you age.

Planning Ahead
Few of us take the time to do the praying, thinking, talking, and acting needed to prepare for the future. Planning for difficult times is particularly hard because it requires anticipating negative possibilities, trying to imagine uncertain, hard-to-face situations, and facing the inevitable end-times of our lives. Planning ahead is practical. Planning ahead is an act of love.

Resources
Each section of the book provides brief background information and refers you to additional materials for in-depth study. The information contained in this book is believed to be accurate, but when expert assistance is required, the services of a competent professional should be sought.

Next Steps

You are urged to complete the forms listing personal, financial, and spiritual matters, and arrange for the execution of any pertinent legal documents. The task may look formidable, but take the first steps now.

Where should you keep documents after they are executed? The originals of your will, any trusts, and durable power of attorney should be kept in your safe deposit box or other secure locations. Originals of health care power of attorney or advance medical directives should be kept at home with copies to your physician and family members. Family members should know the location of the originals.

Most importantly, we suggest you keep copies of important documents and other papers attached to the appropriate pages, noting on each where the original is filed. This will facilitate periodic reviews, at least every two years, and will make "picking up the pieces" a lot easier for members of your family.

Planning ahead is an act of love!

1 Personal and Financial Information

Note: If additional space is needed, use back of form or separate sheet.

A. PERSONAL FAMILY DATA

1. Individual

   Name _____

   Address _____

   _____

   Phone Number _____

   Date and Place of Birth _____

   _____

   Social Security Number _____

2. Spouse or Other Primary Personal Contact

   Name _____

   Address _____

   _____

   Phone Number _____

   (If spouse)

   Date and Place of Birth _____

   _____

   Date and Place of Marriage _____

   _____

   Social Security Number _____

3. Deceased or Prior Spouses (if applicable)
   Name _____
   Address _____
   _____

   Date and Place of
       Marriage _____
       _____

       Divorce _____
       _____

       Death _____
       _____

       Social Security Number _____

4. Survivors (Children or Significant Persons)
   Name _____
   Relationship _____
   Address _____
   _____

   Phone Number _____

5. Pets
   Instructions for Disposition of Pets _____
   _____
   _____

B. PERSONAL SUPPORT DATA
   1. Physician _____
      Address _____
      _____

      Phone Number _____

   2. Attorney _____
      Address _____
      _____

Phone Number_____

3. Accountant/Tax Preparer_____
   Address_____

   Phone Number_____

4. Durable Power of Attorney
   Person Named to Act_____
   Address_____

   Phone Number_____

5. Health Care Declaration/Living Will
   Person Named to Act_____
   Address_____

   Phone Number_____

6. Executor of Your Will_____
   Address_____

   Phone Number_____

7. Trustees of Any Trust for You_____

   Address_____

   Phone Number_____

8. Insurance Agent_____
   Address_____

Phone Number _____

9. Stockbroker _____
   Address _____
   _____
   Phone Number _____

10. Investment Adviser _____
    Address _____
    _____
    Phone Number _____

11. Banker _____
    Address _____
    _____
    Phone Number _____

12. Pension Fund Payer _____
    Address _____
    _____
    Phone Number _____

13. Others to Notify:

    _____
    _____
    _____
    _____
    _____
    _____
    _____
    _____
    _____

C. LOCATION OF IMPORTANT DOCUMENTS

Document	Location
1. Will	
2. Durable Power of Attorney	
3. Advanced Health Care Directive	
4. Trust agreements	
5. Birth certificate	
6. Marriage certificate	
7. Naturalization papers	
8. Adoption papers	
9. Military discharge papers	
10. Social Security card	
11. Medicare card	
12. Medicaid card	
13. Title to real estate property/ mortgage papers	
14. Title to automobiles	
15. Contract for long term care facility, and/or other contracts and legal documents	
16. Inventory of household goods/ personal property (including appraisal and pictures if taken)	
17. Other storage places for important property/documents	
18. Insurance policies	
life	
health	
disability	
automobile	
homeowners	
excess liability	
long term care	
other	

19. Current papers and receipts for filing tax returns _____

20. Income tax returns for last five years and supporting records _____

21. Safe deposit box _____
    Keys _____

22. Other essential keys _____

D. LISTING OF ASSETS AND DEBTS

Assets
(include account number)

Location

1. Checking accounts

2. Savings accounts

3. Money markets and CDs

4. Stocks

5. Bonds

6. Brokerage accounts

7. Mutual funds

8. Trusts for which you are beneficiary

9. Mortgages and other debts owed to you

10. Pension, other retirement plans (including IRAs and Keoghs)

11. Autos, boats, RVs, etc.

12. Primary residence

13. Vacation home

14. Other real estate holdings

    _____

15. Other investments

    _____

    _____

    _____

    _____

    _____

Debts   *Location*

1. Mortgage

    _____

2. Loans

    auto

    bank

    other

3. List of credit cards

4. Persons dependent on you for support

    Name   *Type of support*

2   Health Insurance and Living Arrangements

Note: Figures are as of January 1, 1998. They change annually.

Medical Insurance

Medicare is provided through the Social Security program. It does not cover all costs. Insurance to supplement Medicare is called "medigap" insurance. This supplemental coverage is available through Blue Cross/Blue Shield, the American Association of Retired Persons (AARP), health maintenance organizations (HMOs), and other commercial insurers.

Federal law now limits available medigap policies to ten standardized types. These policies have been developed by the National Association of Insurance Commissioners. Every insurer issuing medigap policies must offer a basic medigap ("core") policy.

During the first six months of eligibility, an insurer cannot reject an applicant or charge more for poor health. Note, however, that neither Medicare nor the medigap policies cover the cost of custodial nursing care.

COVERAGE PROVIDED WHEN MEDICARE IS COMBINED WITH THE CORE POLICY

Medicare	*"Core"*
PART A (Hospital, per benefit period)	(Minimum coverage required by law)
Day 1–60 all but the initial $764 deductible	————————
Day 61–90 all but the $191- a-day co-pay	$191 a day
60 additional days all but the $382- a-day co-pay (one-time reserve)	$382 a day
365 additional days none	all Part A eligible expenses
PART B (Medical expenses)	
$100 deductible (each calendar year)	20% of eligible expenses
not covered	80% of eligible expenses above the $100 deductible

In each benefit period, Medicare Part A covers the following:

1. Inpatient hospital services such as:
   bed (semiprivate) and board
   nursing services and other related services
   use of hospital facilities
   drugs, supplies, and equipment
   medical and surgical services of interns and residents
   certain diagnostic and therapeutic services

2. Extended care services for a specific condition, when skilled care is required on a daily basis and is available only in a nursing home. The patient must have been hospitalized for at least three consecutive days for the condition and admitted to the nursing home within thirty days of release from the hospital. Medicare will cover the entire cost for the first twenty days, then there is a deductible of $95 a day for the next eighty days. After one hundred days Medicare covers nothing.

3. Home health care services when part time or intermittent skilled care is needed and the patient is confined to home and under a physician's care.

A benefit period begins on the first day the patient is hospitalized (provided the hospitalization lasts at least three continuous days) and ends when the patient has received no skilled care for sixty-one days.

The following publications are available:

Guide to Health Insurance for People with Medicare, published by U.S. Department of Health and Human Services and the National Association of Insurance Commissioners.

Medicare: What It Covers; What It Doesn't, AARP publication D13133. (800) 424-3410

Your Medicare Handbook 1997, published by U.S. Health Care Financing or Social Security Administration. (800) 772-1213

Long Term Care Insurance
Since neither Medicare nor Medigap policies cover the cost of long term care whether in a nursing home or at home, other sources are necessary to finance this care. One option is to purchase insurance that covers the cost of nursing home or other long term care.

Nursing home and home care costs are considerable ($50,000 and up per year). Over a period of years these costs could substantially reduce or eliminate the assets of many persons. Long term care insurance can be purchased to cover part or all of the potential cost. The insurance premium depends on three factors: (1) the insurer's age, (2) the amount of coverage, and (3) the number of years.

Choosing the best policy for you is not easy. There are more than 110 different companies writing some form of individual long term care policies. Some provide home health care as well as nursing home care. It is important to consider whether you want coverage for both home and institutional care. Also, it is important to consider the level of care the policy will cover. Typically there are three levels of care: skilled, intermediate, and custodial. Some policies cover skilled care only when ordered by a physician. Whatever policy you choose, it should be guaranteed renewable and not require prior hospitalization.

The following publications are available:

Making Wise Decisions for Long Term Care, AARP publication D12435. (800) 424-3410

Long Term Care Insurance, published by the Health Care Insurance Association of America.

Before You Buy: A Guide to Long Term Care Insurance, AARP publication D12893.

A Shopper's Guide to Long Term Care Insurance, National Association of Insurance Commissioners. (816) 374-7259

How to Choose a Nursing Home

In this book we review several alternative living arrangements that provide health care. Although many people shrink at the thought, in many cases a nursing home is the best solution when long term care is needed.

If nursing home care is required but there are not enough funds available, Medicaid becomes an issue. The eligibility requirements for Medicaid vary depending on whether the individual is married or single. In Pennsylvania (or in whichever state he or she resides), a married couple with one spouse needing nursing home care can have no more than $74,820 in combined assets (excluding their home) and $1,919 in monthly income. A single person can have no more than $3,400 in assets.

Be prepared to spend considerable time choosing a nursing home. From the resources listed below and with some counseling, you should choose three or four that appear to meet your needs, then visit each one, taking time to talk with the staff, the residents, and their families. You should identify the owner and management of the facility and examine their experience record as it relates to any problems cited by regulatory authorities. Not all nursing homes are alike in their ability to treat patients. Some are better equipped to meet the needs of ambulatory patients while others may focus on the needs of specific illnesses such as Alzheimer's disease. Take the time to select the nursing home that best meets your individual needs.

The following publications are available:

Nursing Home Life: A Guide for Residents and Families, AARP publication D13063. (800) 424-3410

Local guides are available from regional health associations and in mid-Atlantic states from the publication *Retirement Living*, (800) 394-9990, or on the Internet at www.retirement-living.com

---

Home Health Care
Home care is a service for the recovering, disabled, or chronically ill person that provides treatment and/or help to effectively function in a home environment. Generally, home health care is appropriate whenever you need

assistance that cannot be easily or effectively provided by a family member or friend, whether the need is short or long term.

Your financial resources should be considered when determining your ability to maintain the home and pay for the in-home services. Medicare, Medicaid, and programs under the Older Adults Act and Social Services Block Grants pay limited amounts for home care. Additionally, private insurance can be obtained which will cover home care (see long term care insurance section). However, most home care is paid for by the individual and his or her family.

If you employ at-home support staff, numerous reporting, tax withholding, and other administrative responsibilities must be satisfied. As an alternative, individuals can contract with an agency that provides in-home companions, nurses, and other appropriate personnel. Many times the cost of in-home health care can exceed that of a nursing home.

The basic services that can generally be provided in the home include

medical and skilled nursing care
speech, respiratory, physical, or occupational therapy
nutrition or dietary services
hospice services for the terminally ill

Personal care or home-maker services are often included in descriptions of home health care, even though the services are not medical in nature. They include assistance with bathing, dressing, eating, and toileting. Community services such as "meals on wheels" and adult day care also play a role in providing at-home living.

A "care manager," usually a nurse or social worker, can be contracted privately or from a home health care agency to evaluate, coordinate, and monitor a variety of services to meet the needs of a particular client.

Life-Care-at-Home is a pioneering concept in home health care. It is being offered in southern Pennsylvania and is similar in some respects to continuing care communities. There are entrance and monthly fees, but they are substantially less than for the life care communities.

Acceptance in the program guarantees a continuum of long term care at home and in nursing homes when needed, for persons who wish to continue living independently in their own homes as long as possible.

For an individual entrance fee (depending on age, the plan chosen, and variable monthly fees), members receive a broad range of health and home-maker services for the rest of their lives. The plan pays a large percentage of the cost for a stay in one of several nursing homes, if needed.

The following publications are available:

A Consumer's Guide to Home Health Care, National Consumers League.

How to Choose a Home Health Care Agency, The National Association for Home Care.

A Handbook about Care in the Home, AARP publication

D955. (800) 424-3410

Miles Away and Still Caring, (for long distance care givers) AARP publication D12748.

Friends Life Care at Home. (215) 628-8964. Internet address: www.friendslifecareathome.com

Care Management—Arranging for Long Term Care, AARP publication D13803.

Staying at Home: Guide to Long Term Care and Housing, AARP publication D14986.

Note: This is a rapidly changing field, so be sure your information is correct.

Is a Life Care Community for You?

Life care or continuing care communities have flourished. A one-time entrance fee, along with a monthly service fee, pay for your apartment or villa, some meals, outpatient health care, and your stay in the on-site assisted living or nursing facility, should you need that level of care. Typically, you must sign a contract that stipulates the terms of your residency.

Entrance fees vary greatly, whether for a studio apartment in a church-related community or a villa in a more exclusive community. Most facilities provide a prorated refund and some facilities return a percentage of the entrance fee if a resident moves or dies within a period of time specified in the contract.

When you apply for residency in a life care community, the management will want assurances that (1) you have sufficient funds to pay the entrance and monthly fees, which may increase substantially over your lifetime and

(2) you have reasonably good health so that long-term skilled care will not be needed immediately. Financial statements and a medical exam are usually required.

On the other hand, you must assure yourself that the operator can provide high-quality care for your lifetime and remain financially sound. Bankruptcies are rare but have occurred among the life care communities. You should review the community's financial statements, reserve account balances, and history of fee increases. Also identify the management of the facility and review their record. Finally, consider the procedure by which residents' complaints are addressed and responded to by management.

Since a decision to enter such a community is a major decision involving your property, estate, financial, and healthcare planning, you should consult with an attorney concerning the long-term admissions contract you will be asked to sign.

The following publication is available:

Not-for-Profit Housing and Care Options for Older People, published by the American Association of Homes and Services for the Aging, which also embodies the accreditation agency for continuing care communities. (800) 675-6253 and on the Internet at www.aahsa.org

---

Hospice Care
The term *hospice*, from the same word root as *hospitality*, was used in early days to describe a place of shelter and rest for weary or sick travelers. The hospice of today provides

pain and symptom management for people for whom active treatment is no longer appropriate.

Usually, to be admitted into a hospice program, the patient's doctor and the hospice medical director must certify that the patient is terminally ill with a life expectancy of six months or less. Something can always be done to provide comfort. Practical assistance and emotional and spiritual support can be provided at a time when patients and their families feel most alone.

When terminal illness strikes, social, psychological, financial, and spiritual issues frequently accompany the physical deterioration. The interdisciplinary team helps the patient and family identify and cope with these issues. The hospice commitment to the family follows through to the bereavement phase.

Hospice care is a benefit under Medicare Hospital Insurance (Plan A) and is primarily delivered in the patient's home under a plan of care established by the patient's attending physician. Medicare covers physician services, nursing care, medical appliances and supplies, outpatient drugs for symptom and pain relief, home health aid and homemaker services, physical and speech therapy, and medical services.

In addition to these professionals, the patient's minister is an important member of the team, as is the dedicated volunteer whose quiet presence, understanding concern, and human touch can be of great comfort to the patient.

Information concerning the hospice program can be obtained from the following sources:

Your physician
Your local hospital

3   Explanation of Pertinent
Legal Documents

Durable Power of Attorney

A durable power of attorney is a document in which you (the "Principal") appoint another person (the "Attorney") to act in your place and on your behalf with regard to managing your assets and personal business issues. The document gives direction to the attorney by listing specifically granted powers as well as any restrictions or limitations on these powers. Unlike a traditional power of attorney, which ceases to be effective if you become incapacitated, a durable power of attorney is effective during periods of incapacity or disability. Thus, a durable power of attorney is an effective way of providing for management of assets during a period of incapacity.

A durable power of attorney is easy to establish. There is great flexibility in the powers and instructions that can be given to the attorney so that the document can be tailored to your circumstances. You can name more than one person to serve as your attorney either jointly (together), severally (one or the other), or as a successor. A power of attorney does not prevent you from handling your affairs but instead provides for the management of your property through the designation of an agent during periods when you cannot or choose not to act. A durable power of attorney can be effective immediately or only under specific conditions. In either case, it is a powerful document and should be kept in a secure location. A power of attorney is terminated by notifying the attorney in writing that it has been revoked. Similarly, your death terminates the attorney's power to act.

Without a valid power of attorney, a guardianship hearing would be required to appoint someone to take control of your assets and use them for your benefit.

A durable power of attorney is the lifetime counterpart of a will. You execute a will to provide for the management and disposition of your assets at death and name an executor to carry out your instructions. A power of attorney provides for the management of your assets during your lifetime and names an attorney to carry out your instructions.

Although there are fill-in-the-blank power of attorney forms, it is important that you have an attorney who is familiar with your estate and the depository provisions of your will. Draft the document to ensure the specific powers and/or limitations contained in your power of attorney correspond with the terms and intent of your will.

Guardianship
A guardianship is a legal relationship in which one person, the guardian, is granted both the responsibility and the authority to make decisions on your behalf if you have been judged by a court incapable of managing your own affairs.

If you are no longer able to handle your affairs, a concerned relative or friend may petition the court of the county in which you live to have a guardian appointed to manage your affairs. The court must hold a hearing and make specific findings of fact before appointing a guardian. If appointed, a guardian must file annual reports with the court. If you regain capacity, a subsequent hearing is required to terminate the guardianship.

The guardianship process is expensive, since an attorney must prepare the petition and represent the concerned person at the hearing. Further, the court may appoint a separate attorney to represent you (the incapacitated individual). If the appointed guardian is not a family member, the court will approve some compensation for services rendered. The process is time consuming and the proceedings are a matter of public record.

If you do not have a valid durable power of attorney and own assets in your own name, a guardianship would be necessary to provide for the management of assets during any period of incapacity.

Health Care Power of Attorney and
Advanced Health Care Declaration

1. Health Care Power of Attorney

All states have statutes that authorize the delegation of powers to an attorney-in-fact (the "Attorney") and list specific powers that may be granted. One of those listed is the power to authorize admission to medical facilities and the power to authorize medical procedures. Specifically, this permits the attorney to apply for your admission to a medical, nursing, residential, or similar facility and to enter into agreements for your care. In addition, this power allows the attorney to consent to medical, surgical, and therapeutic procedures.

The delegation of health care powers can be included in the general power of attorney or granted separately in a health care power of attorney. It can become effective when the document is executed or only under pre-established conditions. When the health care power of attorney is combined with the advanced health care declaration (described below) the person named to make the above-mentioned medical decisions would also make treatment decisions if you are incapacitated and in the advanced stage of a terminal condition or a permanent state of unconsciousness.

2. Advanced Health Care Declaration (Living Will)

All states permit, and you are encouraged to execute, a document termed an advanced health care declaration. Legislation recognizes that all competent adults have a qualified right to control decisions relating to their own medical care subject to certain interests of society such as ethical standards in the medical profession and the protection of human life.

Anyone eighteen years of age or older, and of sound mind, may execute such a declaration. The document must enumerate the kinds of treatment desired or not desired. A blanket or undirected statement such as "no heroic measures" is not adequate. The document is effective only when you are incapacitated and in a terminal condition or in a state of permanent unconsciousness.

As part of the admissions process, hospitals are required to ask if you have executed such a declaration and if you answer in the negative, urge you to do so. However, you should not contemplate such an important decision under the stress of a serious illness or hospitalization. It would be better to consider the issue now and execute a declaration indicating which of the listed treatments you do or do not want. The declaration can be changed at any time but at least it will be in place if a grave medical emergency arises.

Legislation also provides for the naming of a surrogate to make health care decisions when you are incapacitated and in a terminal condition or a state of permanent unconsciousness. However, the surrogate must be given guidance as to the treatment you do or do not wish. If this advanced health care declaration is combined with a health care power of attorney, the surrogate will have the power to make a broader range of medical decisions for you.

Individual churches are urged to offer seminars where a health care power of attorney and advance health care declaration may be executed. We urge you to consider executing such a document and giving a copy to your doctor, pastor, and surrogate.

Will

You should review your will from time to time to ensure that your property will pass to those you seek to favor.

A will is a statement that stipulates the disposition of your property at death. Generally a will must be in writing. In addition, there are other specific requirements that must be met for a will to be recognized by the court. This recognition ensures that your property will be distributed according to your specifications.

If you die without a valid will, the state intestacy laws determine how the property is distributed. Depending on the specific circumstances, these laws generally favor children, a spouse, parents, and even grandparents and their lineal descendants in varying proportions. If there are no relatives within a certain degree, the state takes the property.

Some people believe that if all property is jointly owned with a spouse or child, a will is not necessary. While it is true that property owned jointly as tenants, by the entirety, or with right of survivorship, is not controlled by a will, it is almost impossible to own all property jointly. For instance, personal items such as jewelry are not jointly owned. In addition, joint ownership may result in the eventual payment of unnecessary taxes.

When drawing a will you should consider the gifts you wish to make to family members as well as to charitable organizations that may be important to you, including your church.

Revocable (Living) Trust

A revocable trust is a trust that you create during your lifetime which can be revoked at any time prior to your death. Usually you create the trust by signing a document, contribute assets to fund it, and serve as the initial trustee and beneficiary. You retain control over the management and disposition of the trust assets during your life. The trust should provide for a successor trustee to act should you become incapacitated or upon your death. At death, the successor trustee directs the disposition of the trust assets according to the provisions of the trust instrument. You have the same flexibility to dispose of your assets by means of a trust as you do with a will. Once the trust is created it must be funded in order to be effective. This means that assets must be retitled from your name to that of the trust. Additionally, accurate records must be kept for the trust.

A revocable trust is tax neutral in terms of both estate and income tax. Since you can control the assets, their value is included in your estate for calculating estate tax. The income from the assets must be reported on your income tax return just as if the assets were titled in your own name.

Assets held in a revocable trust, like jointly owned assets and those distributed by beneficiary designation, are not subject to the probate process. Instead they are distributed according to the terms of the trust instrument. Probate affects only assets held in your individual name. These assets are distributed according to your will.

A revocable trust may save attorney's fees for administering an estate but legal fees will be incurred when the trust is established. In addition, the fees for the successor trustee to administer and distribute the assets may approximate executor fees.

The main advantage of a revocable trust is that you have organized your assets, gathering and titling them in the name of the trust, so that if you become incapacitated or die, the successor trustee will have less to do to distribute the assets to your heirs.

Beneficiary Designations in Contracts

It is important to realize that life insurance, IRAs and pension plans are contracts and pass according to the beneficiary designation you stipulate in the contract. Usually you name a primary beneficiary and an alternate who would receive the proceeds if the primary beneficiary predeceases you. The beneficiary designations should be periodically reviewed to ensure that they reflect your current intent.

If you fail to name a beneficiary or all named beneficiaries predecease you, the proceeds of the insurance, IRA, or pension plan will be paid to your estate. Therefore, it is important for your will to contain a residuary clause which provides for the distribution of any assets that may be included in your estate.

The following publication is available:

Tomorrow's Choices, AARP publication D13479. (800) 424-3410

---

4   Spiritual Planning and Resources

"... neither death, nor life, ... nor anything else in all creation, will be able to separate us from the love of God in Christ Jesus our Lord."

Romans 8:38–39

Trust in the love and power of God does not eliminate the grief that accompanies a loved one's death. Recognizing that it is often difficult to plan wisely under emotional stress, the church encourages its members to discuss and plan in advance the arrangements that will be necessary at the time of death. Without such planning, surviving members of the family may have to make decisions at a time when they are shocked and confused.

When preparations are made and discussed with others, survivors are relieved of difficult questions as to what is right and have the satisfaction of knowing that they are doing what the deceased would have wanted. Planning ahead also means that the arrangements and service will express the comfort and hope of the Christian faith fully and without compromise. This book is intended to assist church members in such preparation. Ministers are more than willing to discuss these matters with any who wish to do so.

Practical Considerations

When death occurs, who are the appropriate persons to be called initially?

Your pastors will provide support and guidance. If not present, the deceased's physician or emergency medical personnel should be notified.

What services are supplied by a funeral director?

As many or as few as a family wishes. In addition to various matters having to do with the transportation and disposition of the body, the director will provide the family with copies of the death certificate, the use of the funeral home, rental of cars, the placing of death notices in local newspapers, or the opening of the grave. The funeral director will also need certain information (see Data and Preferences, below).

Is it possible to make funeral arrangements before one's death?

Yes, such pre-planning with your pastor and/or a funeral director of one's choice is now quite common. In many cases, one may even pre-pay all the costs of the services desired. In some instances this could assure the cost of the services being fixed.

What information is contained in a death notice?

The name of the deceased; age and date of death; names of survivors; date, time and place of religious service; designation of memorial gifts (if any).

What information is contained in an obituary?

An obituary contains more biographical information than a death notice. A newspaper does not charge a fee for running an obituary, and it is usually the responsibility of the family to submit it.

What about memorial gifts?

Many families request that in lieu of flowers friends make a contribution to the church or to a favorite charity of the deceased.

What about an autopsy?

Presbyterian doctrine would support an autopsy if it leads to the advancement of medical knowledge or peace of mind for the family.

What procedures are followed in donating one's body (or certain body parts) for medical purposes?

In case of certain organs, consult your local transplant program. For total body donation, contact your local medical school.

What choices are there in the disposition of a body?

Apart from donating it for medical purposes, there are two choices: (1) body burial (or entombment in a mausoleum) or (2) cremation. Once this decision has been made, the funeral director will make all arrangements.

Does state law require that a body be embalmed?

No. It is not necessary in the case of cremation or immediate burial. It is a requirement in most states, for a body held more than twenty-four hours after death.

In the case of cremation, must a casket be purchased?

No. The body can be transported to the crematory in a pine box or other simple container.

What about viewing the body?

Often it is helpful for members of the family to view the body at least once to assist in the process of accepting the fact that death has occurred. This can be arranged at the funeral home or at the time of death.

What happens to the cremated remains?

The urn containing them may be placed in a niche in a columbarium/mausoleum of a local cemetery or buried in the family plot of a cemetery.

What resources are there in coping with grief?

Pastors are available to counsel family and friends in times of death. There are several books available that deal with grief. In addition, support groups help individuals cope with grief.

Data and Preferences

Note: Retain the original of this document, consider giving one copy to pastor to officiate, and one to person chosen to make arrangements at time of death.

1. *Information for death certificate*

   date of birth   _____

   place of birth   _____

   citizenship   _____

   full name—spouse   _____

full name—father	_____
full name—mother	_____
social security number	_____
veteran discharge papers	
with serial number	_____

Note: Request at least 10 copies of death certificate (funeral director will provide).

2. *Friend or relative you wish to oversee arrangements at time of death.*

Name _____

Phone _____

3. *Arrangement preferences* (check appropriate statement and fill in):

( ) Funeral director (if pre-planned or prepaid contract, give location of document)

( ) Cremation with ashes buried or scattered at

( ) Burial in (modest) casket at cemetery (location of deed to plot)

( ) Donation of body to medical school or organs to a transplant program

( ) Information for obituary (insert additional page)

( ) Other arrangements as follows:

Your Name   _____
Date   _____

Religious Services

> "The service on the occasion of death ordinarily should
> be held in the usual place of worship in order to join this
> service to the community's continuing life and witness
> to the resurrection. The service shall be under the direc-
> tion of the pastor. Others may be invited to participate
> as leaders in the service at the discretion of the pastor."
>
> "Directory for Worship," *Book of Order*,
> Presbyterian Church (U.S.A.)

Timing

In most cases a service takes place within a few days of the
death. The main service may precede or follow a brief
committal service at the burial site. Typically, the committal service is attended by members and close friends of
the family.

Location

Usually services are held in a church.

Type of Service

The service may be either a memorial service without the
presence of a casket or urn, or a funeral service where the
casket or urn is present. If a casket is present, it will be

—36—

closed and covered with a white pall in order that the attention of those attending may be directed toward God.

Costs

Most churches intend that costs for a funeral or memorial service on its premises be only what are necessary and minimal. There may be charges to cover custodial services, the organist/soloist fees (if music is a part of the service), and a reception if desired. Exact details are available from the church or the officiating pastor. An honorarium for pastors may be offered at the discretion of the family.

Flowers

Flowers add color and beauty to the service, and remind worshipers of the goodness of God's creation. Ordinarily, one or two flower arrangements are sufficient for the church.

Content of Service

The service is planned by the pastor in consultation with the family. The purpose is to provide comfort and strength to mourners, to give thanks to God for the life of the deceased, and, above all, to bear witness to the hope of Christian faith. It is appropriate for hymns and other sacred music to be part of the service. Music should serve to direct the attention of those attending to the presence and power of God, and enable worshipers to voice their confidence in God's sovereign love. A list of suggested hymns is appended. Scripture should be read and prayers offered. A homily may be preached and words of appreciation may be spoken by the pastor, family members, friends, and colleagues.

Suggested Outline
Funeral or Memorial Service

Organ Prelude

Opening Sentences

Hymn

Invocation

Old Testament Readings/Psalms

Solo

New Testament Readings

Homily

Prayers

The Lord's Prayer

Hymn

Benediction

Organ Postlude

Not everyone will wish to include all of the elements listed here. The use of hymns, for instance, will depend somewhat on the number of people expected for the service. Following the service the family may receive friends at a reception.

Suggestions for Scripture

Old Testament

Job 19:23–27	I know that my redeemer lives
Isaiah 40:1–11, 28–31	Comfort my people
Isaiah 40:28–31	Those who wait for the Lord shall renew their strength
Isaiah 65:17–25	I create a new heaven and a new earth
Ecclesiastes 3:1–15	For everything there is a season

Psalms

Psalm 23	The Lord is my shepherd
Psalm 46:1–5,10–11	A very present help in trouble
Psalm 90:1–10,12	Teach us to number our days
Psalm 103	Bless the Lord, O my soul
Psalm 121	I lift up my eyes to the hills
Psalm 130	Out of the depths I cry to the Lord
Psalm 139:1–12	Whither shall I go from thy Spirit?

Epistles

Romans 8:14–23, 31–39	Nothing can separate us
Romans 14:7–9,10c–12	Whether we live or die, we are the Lord's
1 Corinthians 15:20–26; 35–38, 42–44, 50, 53–58	Death is swallowed in victory
2 Corinthians 4:16–5:1	Visible things are transitory, invisible things permanent
1 Thessalonians 4:13–18	The comfort of Christ's coming
Revelation 21:1–4, 22–25; 22:3–5	A new heaven and a new earth

Gospels

Luke 23:33, 39–43	Today you will be with me in Paradise
John 11:17–27	I am the resurrection and the life

John 14:1–6, 25–27	Let not your hearts be troubled
Matthew 18:1–5,10	The greatest in the kingdom of heaven
Mark 10:13–16	Let the children come to me

Suggestions for Music

Hymns

    (page numbers from *The Presbyterian Hymnal*)

260	A Mighty Fortress Is Our God
543	Abide with Me
339	Be Thou My Vision
526	For All the Saints
473	For the Beauty of the Earth
528	Give Thanks for Life
261	God of Compassion
275	God of Our Life
460	Holy God, We Praise Your Name
138	Holy, Holy, Holy
457	I Greet Thee, Who My Sure Redeemer Art
263	Immortal, Invisible, God Only Wise
447	Lead On, O King Eternal
529	Lord of the Living
555	Now Thank We All Our God
270	O God, in a Mysterious Way
384	O Love That Wilt Not Let Me Go
210	Our God, Our Help in Ages Past
478	Praise, My Soul, the King of Heaven
171	The King of Love My Shepherd Is
175	The Lord's My Shepherd
119	The Strife Is O'er, the Battle Done

The *Presbyterian Hymnal* also has metrical settings to many psalms. Several of these are appropriate for use in a funeral or memorial service.

Other possibilities include the playing of hymns or, where the family has a special musical interest, major organ works such as Bach preludes and fugues or works of César Franck.

Personal Requests for Service

Note: Retain the original of this document; consider giving one copy to the pastor who is to officiate and one to the person chosen to make arrangements at time of death.

( )   I wish to have a funeral service
( )   I wish to have a memorial service

( )   I wish the service be held in the
           ( ) chapel
           ( ) sanctuary
           ( ) other

Preferred minister to officiate at service:

In lieu of flowers contributions should be sent to:

Suggestions for Service:
    (Your selections of hymns, scripture readings, organ music from those listed herein.)

Your Name _____

Date _____

An Affirmation of Faith

Death often seems to prove that life is not worth living, that our best efforts and deepest affections go for nothing.

We do not yet see the end of death.

But Christ has been raised from the dead, transformed and yet the same person.

In his resurrection is the promise of ours.

We are convinced the life God wills for each of us is stronger than the death that destroys us.

The glory of that life exceeds our imagination but we know we shall be with Christ.

So we treat death as a broken power.

Its ultimate defeat is certain.

In the face of death we grieve.

Yet in hope we celebrate life.

No life ends so tragically that its meaning and value are destroyed.

Nothing, not even death, can separate us from the love of God in Jesus Christ our Lord.

From "A Brief Statement of Faith," *Book of Confessions,* Presbyterian Church (U.S.A.)

5   Values History/Ethical Will

This form provides an opportunity for you to write down your values, wishes, and preferences in a number of areas of your life. Your personal relationships, your overall attitude toward life, your thoughts about illness, marriage, friendship, and faith are all important aspects of your life that can be preserved for your loved ones by completing this form. We have found that people are doing this and their children welcome it.

You are encouraged to be candid and clear with your statements and to share the process of completing this document with your close friends or family. Some of this may not apply and you may want to add information.

1. My epitaph in one sentence:

2. The following three people influenced me most:

3. I have enjoyed the following activities:

4. I am happy to be alive because:

5. The most important lesson I have learned is:

6. The formative events of my life were:

7. My attitude toward death and dying:

8. My attitude toward life-threatening illness:

9. The social causes for which I would like my loved ones to feel a sense of responsibility are:

10. Some of the scripture passages that have meant the most to me are:

11. The following is a brief description of the circumstances of my early life (birth to age 21):

12. My definition of a life well-lived:

13. My personal statement of faith:

14. Marriage is . . .

15. Children are . . .

16. Friendship is . . .

17. Other words for my loved ones: